Not a Monster

Claudia Guadalupe
Martínez

Illustrated by
Laura González

ini Charlesbridge

In the murky waters of a canal, at the edge of a ciudad that was once a great empire, sits an egg.

egg

jelly

Inside that egg is a rare thing,
a so-called water monster,
but it is Not a Monster.

Eyes, a mouth, a tail, and long fins form.

Three pairs of branquias **rojas** take shape.

gills

It hatches, but it is still
Not a Monster.

It is a tadpole that swims
under la luna **blanca**.

It sprouts patas **grises** that stretch out into the water.

These four limbs are long, with thin toes.

Then its color darkens. It is
un rayo **negro** that flashes by.

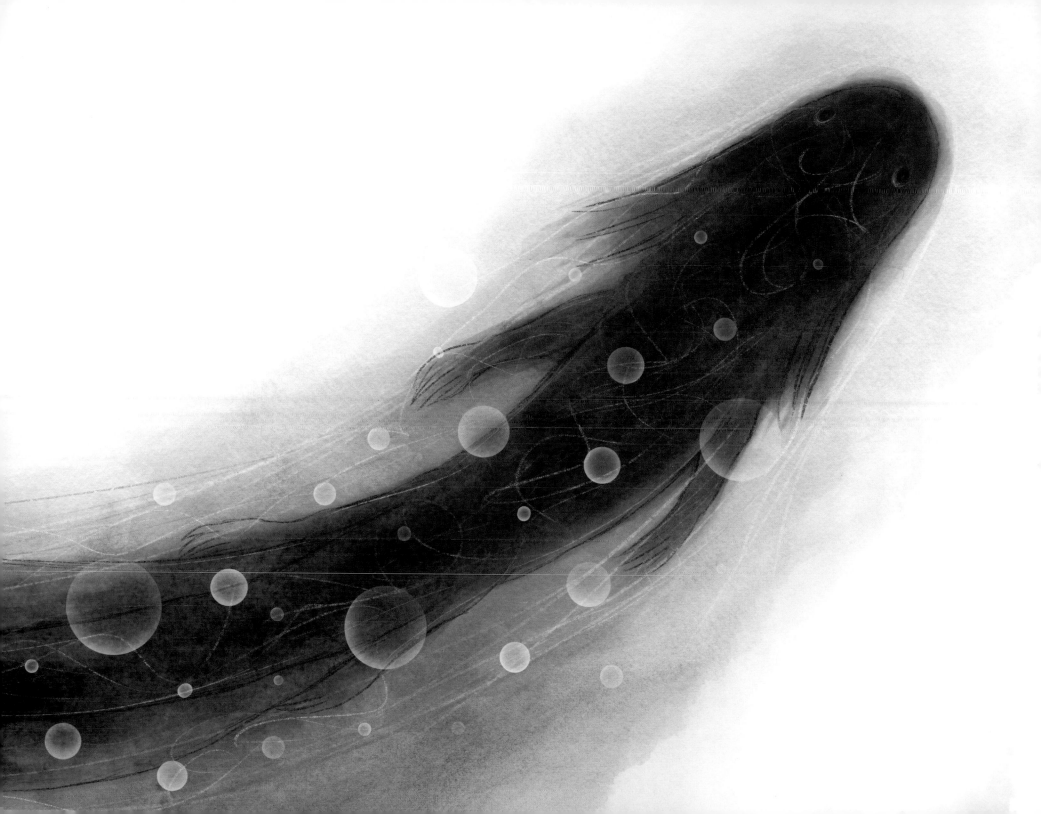

It escapes the hungry carpa **amarilla** that eats everything in sight.

It is safe.

It looks for food among the roots of los lirios **rosados.**

It feasts on insects and small fish that it finds among the water lilies.

It rests under la chinampa **verde**, a floating garden. It is now full grown, but it is still Not a Monster.

It is an axolotl—a salamander
that will never lose its gills
and fins like other salamanders.

A second axolotl swims close by.
Its tail points up. It nudges.
This is a mating dance.

The next morning, the Not a Monster clings to una cáscara **café**. The piece of bark is where it lays its eggs.

A couple of amigos row their chalupa **morada** along the water. They search with eager eyes, guided by the stories their abuelos have told them.

The abuelos say the canals were once a great lago **azul**, with water so blue it was hard to tell where the lake ended and the sky began.

The abuelos say one day the Aztec god of monstrous things jumped into the lake and became an axolotl.

The abuelos say axolotls
thrived in those waters.
As the years passed, people
polluted the canales.

The axolotls began to disappear, and when the last sol **anaranjado** sets and the creatures are gone, it will be the end of paradise.

The amigos return day after day to clean the water. Neighbors help them clear the overgrowth of water lilies and other weeds. They fish out plastic bags and bottles.

One day, one of the amigos points. "Huevos de ajolote!" There is a burst of life as the eggs begin to hatch. The axolotls have not disappeared yet.

There is hope for paradise.

Maybe that is why
the axolotl smiles.

VOCABULARY

ABUELOS: grandparents
AMIGOS: friends
BRANQUIAS: gills
CANALES: canals
CARPA: carp
CÁSCARA: bark or brown shell
CHALUPA: canoe or small boat
CHINAMPA: floating garden
CIUDAD: city
HUEVOS DE AJOLOTE: axolotl eggs
LAGO: lake
LIRIOS: lilies
LUNA: moon
PATAS: legs
RAYO: ray
SOL: sun

COLORS

AMARILLA/AMARILLO: yellow
ANARANJADA/ANARANJADO: orange
AZUL: blue
BLANCA/BLANCO: white
CAFÉ: brown
GRIS: gray
MORADA/MORADO: purple
NEGRA/NEGRO: black
ROJA/ROJO: red
ROSADA/ROSADO: pink
VERDE: green

A Spanish noun uses an article: el/la/los/las mean "the," and un/una/unos/unas mean "a."

AUTHOR'S NOTE

The word axolotl (ak-suh-LAHT-ul) is associated with the Aztec god of monstrous things, Xolotl. While the word means "water monster" in the Indigenous language of Nahuatl (nah-WAHT-ul), the axolotl is also sometimes called a water dog or Mexican walking fish.

The axolotl is actually a salamander. Many other kinds of salamanders undergo metamorphosis as they mature, losing their gills, developing eyelids, and growing larger lungs. The larvae of axolotls grow into adults without metamorphosis. They remain gilled, keeping other juvenile features like larval skin and fins. Unlike those other salamanders, who return to the water only to lay their eggs, adult axolotls are aquatic—though they do have small lungs.

Axolotls are commonly bred in captivity. Many people, including me, keep axolotls as pets. They are also often used in scientific research because they breed easily in captivity and can regrow body parts. While there are plenty of axolotls in labs and home aquariums, the natural population is also very important because it contributes to genetic diversity. A genetically diverse species is less susceptible to disease.

Unfortunately, axolotls are endangered in their natural habitat: the canals of Xochimilco (soh-chee-MEEL-koh) in Mexico City. Their biggest threats are invasive fish species and humans, who pollute the water in multiple ways. Local residents illegally dump raw sewage, and treated water that contains heavy metals is pumped into the canals from nearby communities.

Sirius (top) and Bellotrix (bottom), the author's pet axolotls

Xochimilco was designated a World Heritage site by the United Nations Educational, Scientific, and Cultural Organization (UNESCO) in 1987, and there has been no shortage of preservation plans over the years. However, these plans remain incomplete and underfunded.

You can help by supporting the cleanup of the axolotl's natural habitat through organizations like Movimiento de Jóvenes por el Agua (MOJA), the World Wildlife Foundation, Earthwatch, and El Laboratorio de Restauración Ecológica. Another way to help is to spread the word to your friends, family, school, and community about why it's so important to protect wild axolotls.

To Lui, for fighting the good fight—C. G. M.

En memoria de Jaime Gallegos—L. G.

Published by Charlesbridge
9 Galen Street, Watertown, MA 02472
(617) 926-0329 • www.charlesbridge.com

Library of Congress Cataloging-in-Publication Data
Names: Martínez, Claudia Guadalupe, 1978– author. | González, Laura, 1984– illustrator.
Title: Not a monster / Claudia Guadalupe Martínez; illustrated by Laura González.
Description: Watertown, MA: Charlesbridge, [2023] | Audience: Ages 3–7 | Audience: Grades
    K–1 | Summary: "An axolotl egg hatches and matures in the Xochimilco canals in Mexico
    City, the only natural habitat of these unique salamanders that spend their lives in water."
    —Provided by publisher.
Identifiers: LCCN 2022013058 (print) | LCCN 2022013059 (ebook) | ISBN 9781623543037
    (hardcover) | ISBN 9781632899446 (ebook)
Subjects: LCSH: Axolotls—Juvenile literature. | Rare amphibians—Juvenile literature.
Classification: LCC QL668.C23 M37 2023 (print) | LCC QL668.C23 (ebook) | DDC 597.8/58—
    dc23/eng/20220520
LC record available at https://lccn.loc.gov/2022013058
LC ebook record available at https://lccn.loc.gov/2022013059

Printed in China
(hc) 10 9 8 7 6 5 4 3 2 1

Illustrations created in traditional media and Photoshop
Hand-lettering of title by Laura González
Text type set in Aunt Mildred by MVB Design
Printed by 1010 Printing International Limited in Huizhou, Guangdong, China
Production supervision by Jennifer Most Delaney
Designed by Diane M. Earley